ERIATA ON MARBLE
(book of running lines)

Eriata Oribhabor

Copyright © 2016 **Eriata Oribhabor**

Something for Everybody Ventures

(*Somtin fo Evribodi Vensho*)

ISBN: 978-978-955-203-0

All rights reserved.

This book may not be reproduced, stored in a retrieval system or transmitted in whole or in part, in any form or by any means, electronic, mechanical, photocopying, recording, or otherwise, without the prior written permission of the author, except where permitted by law.

Published by:

Something for Everybody Ventures (SFEV)

Surulere, Lagos, Nigeria

Tel: +2348100091760

Email: edbabor@gmail.com

Facebook: https://facebook.com/oribhabor

Website: www.poetsinnigeria.org.ng

Product of SFEV, Nigeria

Contents

Dedication 4
Acknowledgement 5
ERIATA ON MARBLE 6

Dedication

To my father Prince Eriata Idoni Oribhabor who burnt candles at both ends to give me and my siblings qualitative education.

Acknowledgement

God's hands on Eriata Idoni Oribhabor,
my dad,
glow in me,
reverberating creative effusions
inspiration to friends around the world.

Appreciations to Him
and him,
Watching and guiding my forays,
keeping words;
for justice.

Gabriel Ehijie (ArcAngel),
Kolade Olanrewaju Freedom,
Looked through my running lines,
Eriata on Marble.

On marble cast,
these words will, tested times glow
tomorrow's perspective today.

Eriata Oribhabor
Lagos, Nigeria

Eriata Oribhabor

ERIATA ON MARBLE
(book of running lines)

Eriata on Marble

This devil is white
He has a black hair

This angel is black
He is all-white dressed

Angels and devils never meet
They held a lively ball yesterday

This place of many faces
Lining without a place

Angels don't reside here
Devils don't live here

Eriata Oribhabor

Raindrops are not drops of pain
Showers of pain run on every lane

Streets are lined with billboards of shame
One shows the governor dressed to the teeth

Who is oblivious of the new fashion in town?
Only a clown wouldn't recognize a big fat clown

Whoever risks not wearing the governor's bowl
hat,will answer to his political rave

The governor's wife fell ill yesterday
Only her haters won't visit her today

What's the meaning of stupidity?
Not dancing the governor's dance.

Must the sun rays touch every home?
Must life's bounties rain in every domain?

Who says the "best way" to live isn't
Cornering "best corners" for future corners?

I wouldn't speak of cleanliness unseen
I would seek for needles in bras tags

Eriata on Marble

The story of a season is the season
The message of a season is its reason

The *Iroko's* drum is heard once a year
Big masquerades come scarce

At the rendering of the state's address
Bowler hats will paint the skies

Traditional dancers will display culture
Tradition will on muddied waters pour

Don't owners of rivers beg for fish?
Don't owners of waters drink spittle?

Would you rather walk on steady waters
Or dance in sun posted from foreign quarters?

May I tell where from I come?
May I speak heart of pain I bear?

These lines mustn't rain another rain
Vain sentiments and emptiness

I come from hidden backyards
Shared plated plates of ignominy

Eriata Oribhabor

I cannot connect now; I am told
Must wait for the coming clear coast

What power questions hands
Feeding blinds with connectivity?

Where is the bite of a toothless dog
Howling self-giant to a din?

What do you take me for, he asks
Do you really know me, he thumps

Memory print says he is a goat
Roaming the wilderness of filth

Fanciful faces of sentiments
Reel of fulfilments of failures

Some one says, "all is well"
"God is in control", another says

Not the God of equity
He is love and equity

Eriata on Marble

One word. One sentence. Tenses
Words. Words. Sense and senses

Word train moves on punchlines
Over tea cups served hot burning

Not wheel reinventing
On the fire of a friend riding

His flows, worthy flows
Washing ills forced down throats

One with a hat of worn embroidery
Says, he knows all about the country

Born to rule and rule for life
Harmony on radio and television

One with a cap of colonial extraction
Says, he holds the aces, wasted in all

He talks of ruler ship in hushed tones
It landed on his laps, muzzled out.

"Agbada" has its birthplace in my place
Others are mere copy cats

Destined to reinvent the English language
Illiterates will never rule over us

Eriata Oribhabor

We mustn't on same arena, dance
Less, read as one bush family

Did you know when education came to my
country? While others cursed it, we embraced it?

Can't you see you have an accent?
Can you represent us outside of this place?

I will bathe you clean with the showers of accents
and leadership
Prove that the one with tribal marks mustn't come
near power

I will speak the politics of the regions when things
never worked
Prove that today's political parties outshine that of
the regions

I am here to rearrange the fates of tomorrow
Blind your heads with modern facilities

I will reposition the fortunes of my people
I am not a politician

Eriata on Marble

Not when a story hits one belt below
Not when tears unceasingly flow

I see it when cries pace in raving soars
Like served *"akamu"* soured garnished

Not when held by the jugular
With rail lines wasting in one's heart

I figure it whenever talks rent the air
No intention to impress the sun's fairness

Not when night and darkness roll
Like salt and fresh waters horn-locking

Now, stories wing stories
Telling the telling parts of our world.

Eriata Oribhabor

I see it in countless prisms
I see it in incessant road patches

I see it when the openness of failures
Is dry-cleaned or laundered futile

I see it in signboards of shame planted
Bold on the streets of upturned hopes

I see it run miles on consciences
Leaving generations of potholes

I see it as stone from a careless fling
A palpable wiz that falls in a market buzz

I see it as oil soiling the finger
Cancer veering uncontrollably so

Did you hear what I see?
Did you see what I hear?

Eriata on Marble

Tell me the story of your pain
Tell me stains raining as gains

Tell me the meaning of our history
Washed down the street of Federalism

Tell me the crossroad of our meet
Standing without a feet

Tell me hands of meticulous reign
Arm-twisted into a union of forlorn hope

Tell me refurbishment of rail lines
Speaking same old wine

Tell me changes at the marketplace
Heralding you from abroad

Tell me stories of your long absence
And the place for new thinking in this place

Tell me the state of the clock's hand
Tell me the heart of the clock's state

Eriata Oribhabor

Tell the wind stories of unbundling
From stables of high wired rumblings

I see you dance the dance of yesterday
Will you ever sip the honor of our embrace?

Mount the canoes and speak to the mangroves
Beautiful poisons smell the blood of your hands

Mount the backs of horses and speak to the deserts
You will bathe the cries of wasted innocents

Come to the corners of our homes
Community meetings are filled with moving bones

Hold yourself and speak reality
Less you be consumed by today's music

Eriata on Marble

Did you see the last compromise?
Any difference from the running wise-ness?

Recall its grand entry?
Any difference from the past?

Is the outpouring of hope anew new?
Any newness in yesterday's new?

How is yesterday playing in your head?
Is music crispy clear in your heart or hushed hogwash?

Ever wondered a line of demarcation?
How palpable are altercations feigned?

Are our cities not running as villages?
Are villages not burning into hamlets?

Not questions!
Not answers!

No villages!
No cities!

Eriata Oribhabor

I am not promises *"calabashed"* in calabashes
I am not "piped" dreams running blind
in pipelines of huge failures

I am promise calling for promising hands
I am today's brightness and silver lining

I am not costumes of traditions hung at
village squares across our land
Not politics for self against self

I am a proud "selfie" of myself
Standing bright for all

I am not the chewing stick spitting aching blood of yesterday
I am a generational hope of witty lines for all

I am not the seed of a greedy father who bogeyed
on the planes of focus
I am weaned from thorns and thickets of simplicity

I am not the failure prophesized
A standing success of all sizes

Of all sides,
We collapse as a side

A side of a dot
A dot of a side

Did you hear my voice yesterday?
Don't tell me how husky it bells

Did you hear a voice laced by lapels of confident diction?
Could you spot its tribe?

Didn't you hear me speak of sentiments painted on the screens of our heads?
Did meaning rhyme with message?

Did the drums of order and focus resonate with them?
Will you join to the house of reason?

Didn't we plan to meet at a meeting point smoking true changes?
Did we promise to match promise with sincerity?

Can you reconcile my voice with the moment?
What did you hold to show the moment?

This moment is daring...daring moments
This daring times...times daring

Blaring horns...horns blaring
Horns blaring...blaring horns

Eriata Oribhabor

Tell me where I got it mixed up
Tell me where to key a new start up

Ever wondered power in cursive lines of old?
And its golden web in the cyber world?

Did you know that the milky teeth of yesterday cracked bone
And stands awed in the weakness of today's tone.

Tell me how we got it fondled in bundles of untold waste
Tell me where stand our pride lost in the depths of Corruption

Did you hear the loudness of my voice yesterday?
Was tomorrow's voice coined?

Tell me...come tell me...
Old fat truths...tell me...

How did your fathers brainwash you against us
Can you see the readings in lines of selfish abuse?

How did your mothers fan the embers of hate?
Can you read its failing lines?

Can't you see?
Can't you read?

Eriata on Marble

Tomorrow, I will make embrace with your city long visited
With you, I will warm hug your streets and beauties

Looking forward to an eye ball to ball talk
To unbundle selves for a wagging country

None tells us truth's other side smoking dry
Only truth raising bars of oneness

None holds back our clock
Fixing fits and starts

We shall meet at the boundary of pain and happiness
Darkness, as failure, light as success' brightness

Promises made must be loudly kept
And darkness blown to dazes bright

My arrival bell for happiness will sound
Come with friends to drink in rounds

Bits, parts and pieces of me, served
As sprawling pieces of greatness

Yes...yes...
Say yes...

Eriata Oribhabor

When last did you see a free platform?
By your window, hangs one as stage

When last did you see a cultural festival of teens?
They come free in different colors

When last did you hear of a wasted generation?
We were warned by a guru who saw all in a cringing mire

When last did a chalk write for your eyes?
We use them only on Qui sticks

In the labyrinth of failure lies success
A maze is a maze so identified and labelled

Stretch your hand from your window and tell the warmth you feel
Plant a crop in your room and tell the magic you see

Get me a cup of water
Waters of heavens flow here

Get me honey...get me money
Our streets are awash with honey

Come...come with me to my home
Home of peace and happiness

When will our story change for the change we hold to our chests?
Wondering clean granted yonder lands of glistering floors...

When will our story change from road patches and drain clearings?
Will sincerity of purpose compliments outpourings of the mouth?

When will our story change from pulpits and prayer grounds,
growing congregations and worshippers,
selfish gains and recklessness,
ceremonials packaged by studs for gods?
Where are God fearing leaders?

When will our story change from mere symbols and totems to meaningful focus driven by merit for development?

When will our story change from art for art sake, politics of bread and butter, to art for positive reorientation for societal uplift?
Creativity will feed brains and keep mouths rocking activities

No sentiments of religion and tribe saying; enough is enough
Not snuffed to death with a brazing maze of madness of political regression

Eriata Oribhabor

I am done with poetry...
Yes...I am poetry-done

I am up for the streets
Yes...I am street-poet ready

I am hopping with the time
Yes...Not my kind of time

I am pain strained
Yes...some need flogging

I am on the road...the road spot
Yes...spotting love and equity

I am done with poetry
I am poetry done for the streets

Eriata on Marble

You are wont saying little difference
Counting in swaying million matters

Distance of space are paces summed
Coming in torn rags or worthy sums

Essence of time is wine and foods
Sticklers for the mundane

Steal in bungling sufficiency and build houses,
every town, every city, blind to the hilt

Hard earned paths of greats are tiny dots
To all and sundry, the wild is blazingly open

Mindless mills of mongers are killer gongs
Ripping people and cities in sweeping finishing

How these things play, we see
How these things beat, we hear

Roll out the drums, let the people know
Roll out the drums with a seat for yesterday

Today's judgement
Lies in the presence of yesterday

Eriata Oribhabor

This muddy terrain is God-given
Our habitat is all-given

Beautiful river-ways of poisoned creeks
Run smelly rings in river communities

Upland-deserts are gold mines...
wells of happiness
Trans-Saharan trade is history...
only a handful want to hear

Children roam the dusts of shame...
fall outs of failed leadership
Look up to the hands of heaven...
reason constant in all

Story tellers of our world are going
A blueprint of going raves sit large
in the hearts of killing killers

Creeks, rivers and mangroves are gold-mines
Deserts harbor wells of happiness from time

Untapped bounties lie fallow
Rivers of water dry shallow

People....people...just people
Land...land...all land...land

Eriata on Marble

Lend a hand of peace, justice and equity
Our land's greenery is rich

Lend a face of truth and reality
Mullahs, Imams, Sheiks, Men of God,
Deacons and Elders of pretentious vineyards will keep their truth and join the reality band

Drop a pint of honesty seasoned for progress and development
Our streets will come paved with adornments of beauty,
sanity and hope for a better tomorrow

Sound out the people...
you will feel the pulse of a citizenry fed with wants not needs
You will stop giving stamps of authority to criminals roaming wide with claps from filthy hands

Do you mind a further down this reality ride for society?
You will jump not at conformity built on a ruinous norm

Write and tell the lines, wine and dine on them
But stop not telling yourselves the time to unbundle your hearts,

your whole on the streets with banners posting calls for genuine change

Do you mind a drift or shift from the maddening lot of conformers for bread and butter?
On open squares of life, come and spit the venom in you...
venomous ones appreciate nothing less

Maimed are we...bruised and maimed
Reason...disunity for their unity

Hanging...

Eriata on Marble

Mosquitoes rule in my community
We provide for them daily to have our way

Did you hear the dog bark yesterday?
He was fed fat with our hard earned money to keep him at bay

My neighbor's hands may not be as strong as mine
- all fingers are not equal
Must his children hawk their future
on the streets of mindless traffic jams?
Are they not being pursued from pillar to post for a fee?

A signpost bearing government's seal says;
"Hawking is an offence. Offenders are liable to go to jail"
Government "workers" work with hawkers for their pockets

Another one says; "Don't urinate here. Offenders will be arrested"- Police
A policeman cleans the pole on which the signpost is hung with his urine

"STOP WORK" is a bold warning asking you to come
and start necessary settlements at the office of the owners
of Stop Work and Start Work
A temporary threat.

Eriata Oribhabor

Work must start again.
Buildings won't stop collapsing

This country is collapsing
Leaders are groping

Eriata on Marble

A young man walks up the stage and ask;
why should an audience drown
in the personality of a speaker and not his message?
Criminals walk the streets with pomp and splendor
decorated with expensive chieftaincy titles

A student couldn't speak two straight sentences
without additional "pidgin" imports
He must speak the English language of his colonizers.
His teachers are neither in the class nor the farms.

Where are figures of speech in these lines?
They are locked open in senses they exude

Where is the one called imagery?
I am not used to forcing forgery

Lend me your voice of poetic intuition
I am serious...be serious for an action

We can transform the transformers
who lost their thinking caps taking
electric transformers of government
to private homes across our country

What imagery?
What poetry?

Forgery is the word
The word is criminality

These lines running will run the nooks and crannies of our consciences

These lines will pounce crazy bald heads and buckets of waterlogged kleptocracy

These lines will ruin the ruinous laying venomous mines on the way of a people

These lines will open wraps of sincerity for a roll of Renaissance

These lines will cease the Oligarchy and Dream killers across our sphere

These lines will wake up many day and night with hopeful messages

These lines are running fires of Truth, Justice and Equity

These lines are condiments firing our nation's engine

Eriata on Marble

When the death of 'my father'
Was whispered in the recesses
Of his ilk power wielders
Streets were not awash
With songs of war.
His drummers drunk had regained
Their state...awaiting not his burial
But the final day

When the burial of 'my father' was
announced, his Kinsmen had
Neither gongs nor paid criers
To feign passage ceremonials.
Wagging tongues of pain hung
On our compounds awaiting
Final reports of his sojourn
In the land of glass houses
Built from our brows and blood

When the remains of 'my father' arrived
The entry port to our communities,
He was caught in an aimless walk
Of soliloquy...neither graced
With pomp nor embellished
by accoutrements
Of power boasts of shame
Thrown around for self
At the city of feigned unity

When the carcass of 'my father' was
Laid to rest, he rose to speak

Eriata Oribhabor

Of his days, when "men were men"
And his deceptive mode was
Activated for his sharp tongue
To riot run left spaces
For the pleasure of empty ears
Awaiting the departure of one who
Came, Saw and Misled his people

When the story of dancing boats
and senseless ceremonies will be said,
betrayals would have expanded
our rivers of escaping fishes,
Our children shall wage
Wars in blameful rivers of blood

When the story of a Delta overran
by rampaging "internal colonizers"
will be told,
Bad Chiefs and Bad Cultists
shall dominate,
Good Chiefs and Good Cultists
would have little ground to
launch groundbreaking attacks
against themselves

When the story of Dead Towns
and Dead Cities
shall grace our courts,
Lords and Lordships,
Kings and Queens,
Kings and Kingships,

Eriata on Marble

Princes and Princesses,
Red bloods and Blue bloods,
Will roam as outcasts
In their homes

When the Spirit of a people rise beyond
The colors and contours of sentiments,
Servant leadership would have won
By dint of openness and sincerity.
Dead Towns and Dead Cities
will rise and boom

Eriata Oribhabor

The city of my community is now its village
The village of my community is lost

Pills of sweetness are bitter labor dozes
Sweetness of sweetness is the bitter of tales

Running streams head for rivers
Creeks meander for the streams
Streams and rivers disappearing...
Rivers going...

Water splashes, deep roves,
fading banks, dancing stilts...
Enough space for coming ceremonies

Who tells my people that while they sing and dance
on their sorrows,
their wealth is shared in glass houses around the
country and the world?

Who drinks the sweetness of bitter
in packaged sweetness thinking
it's not bitterness?
Blinds lacking foresight
of big pictures

The city of my community is now its village
The village of my community is lost

Eriata on Marble

These beggars are not our brothers
Here to defile innocent spaces

These beggars are not our sisters
Stealing from different corners

This is a strict place...
old and new are "licensed" to have
children as their "hands" could carry
Customs and traditions are dead...
our religion talks the walk

Is there a truth different
from that told
in huddled prayer places?
What was your first experience
with the "book"?
I will tell a thousand and one
Verses told from the days of
our forefathers

What do you know
about marriages and wives?
I will award you a wife to build
Your harem
But you must stand up
for truth and justice
as told by the "book"
and forefathers who tasted
"books" in their "originals"

These beggars are not our brothers and sisters
They are foreigners handy at needy times

Eriata Oribhabor

The aroma of poetry tastes like honey
Its sweetness comes scented like
Flowers everyone desires.
It sips in killing waves
Taking one on rides across
Country and Oceans
In bold lines

The honey of poetry smells like
Smiles of beautiful brides only
Deserving ones should behold
Coming like the presence
of hairy looking damsels
Whose shyness isn't weakness
But stamps of warmness
piercing faculties
sounding colours
Of goodness

The titles of poetry across our space
Are lines well-crafted for times
In all places without a band
Of fiddle second of loose
foreign hairs bereft of drive
and natural content.
Their crafter's edge knows no bound
And whenever they walk pass,
You wonder the stuff
They are made

The aroma of poetry is as sweet

Eriata on Marble

As the face of the lady you met for the
Very first time...sounding like the
Sister you longed to meet,
Daughter you cherished to the hilts,
An old thoroughbred friend...
a pretty faced Gazelle ...
the aroma of poetry deciphers
the beauty of hearts

The aroma of poetry sends many on
Compulsory sleepless nights
With itchy fingers clutched to handhelds
Running punches within confines
Of keypads linking limitless confines.
And when it reaches high fine times
Of unceasing flows, the taste
Of sleep loses its meaning

The aroma of poetry was a wand
and pride preserve of sages...
Now a gift to ages across our land,
It lends hope and meaning;
it's the Queen of the night brightening
atmospheres all day long
Standing on bare and hairy chests
Telling the essence of tiny and robust
Boobs and how they make sense in
Every sense because the Lord God
Made them all

The aroma of poetry is for the strong

and fickle minded smelling
like no other;
it's from the wild of creativity...
everyone could tap,
not all would identify,
Reached best at moments odd
like when lights are deliberately
switched off for an ambiance
projecting lighted rooms
for willing actors to see
And act right

Eriata on Marble

From Kaduna through Jos,
Bauchi to Gombe down to Adamawa,
a beautiful story of "industrial revolution"
awaits doubting tourists
Legacies of founding fathers beg
for paint and brush

Want a brush of the growing influence
of financial crooks sucking the breath
of genuine leaps in all?
Who next will be decorated with
The colors of the Emirate?

Kingdoms and Emirates...
traditional and religious "evils"
fervent protectors of cultures
and dictates of religion
Who dares otherwise is an outcast
To be "Again Borned"
Or "stoned-bound" in the open

"Boko Haram...band of political traitors
wanting an upstage of the polity,"
So we are stuffed tired.
Leadership statements come best
By arm-twisting
Painful affairs of today,
have nothing to do with yesterday's
faux pas

Eriata Oribhabor

Today, a Man of God
Barks like our neighbor's dog;
"wo...wo...gbraa...die...wo...wo..."
Men of God don't bark...they only shout
Praises at God...proof of piety deserving
His stamp to knock down the devil...

Dare you say our Man of God barks at God?
He is God's representative on earth?

Holy Ghost fire will rain on these
Outpourings of blasphemy running
Us over...down… down...down over...
Who says our God is not a big God?
He will fight our battles...
Praise Master Jesus...

The Ghost of Jesus roams here...
He died for us all...forgotten?
I know him not...he died for his people
...not me...no...not me...

You abuse His Majesty God this way?
Is God Jesus? Is Jesus God?

The Man of God must hear this
None but him must hear this.

Eriata on Marble

Welcome to a new day...
Footsteps sounded convivial exchanges...
"Kantin Safe" was a constant

We breathed the sound and smoke
of textile engines
My city's blood flows from them
New "political development" made them
Comatose whole

We saw it coming from different sacks
Our wives went mad
"Government is coming out with a bailout
hamlets will change to villages
dividends of democracy will flow on the streets",
we were told

Importation of textiles has been cornered
by a gang who must hand power
to their son in-laws and blind loyalists
Survivors roam the streets for menial handouts

Our score card is awesomely dead
Zamfara Textile Mill - dead
Fine-Tex was fine but - dead
Kaduna Textile Mill was a signature - dead
Once famous Asaba Textile Mill - dead
All-Textiles Nigeria - dead
Countless workers - dead
Economy - dead

Our textile engines will sound again
Our dead will yell their stories

Eriata Oribhabor

I am a Community leader leading
my people aright to oil companies...
they must see the color and beauty of oil...
with crumbs, will I wash them as priceless gifts,
Cartons of sardine from United Kingdom
are passports to future crumbs of
packaged pain cocksure
Our people love good things...

I am an Elder in my Church;
fastest growing congregation of children
of God on earth, happiest souls ready for rapture
foretold,
heaven is mine to make
My heavenly home will take me there...

I am anointed to hold the gavel;
a Sheik of reputable standing said so
when I was born, my Imam confirmed it
my great grandfathers ruled over the corners of our
space
My mandate is clear; build on servitude
with digital ink

I am the Chief whose word is law;
I hold my town in my palms...
youths grovel at my feet...
I know my way with "militants",
If I sneeze, Company CEOs cough,
I don't care a hoot about poets;
Like Ministers, they are noise makers…

Eriata on Marble

My town isn't the biggest clown around

Don't tell me about Biafra
I was at the forefront 45years ago
when men were men
What else have I not seen?
If we couldn't sail the seas in our time,
who in this age of internet would cross
our rivers not closing his eyes?
Don't tell me about Biafra...
it will not rise in my time...
over my dead body...
will I join a senseless protest

Biafra will rise again...
Nigeria will rise again...

Eriata Oribhabor

Yesterday, a father killed his son
Bound for head hunters
and killers' markets

Today, a boy squeezed life out
of his father who gave him "life"
Human flesh may be tastier
than beef...who knows what?

Frantic knocks pounded
the booth of a car...
a Vulcanizer heard it right
But the car owner turned deaf ear;
a child thief neck deep
in child trafficking business
She is called Big Mummy!

Business is growing here
Kidnapping is quick business
Lie telling is a way of life;
Politics is alive -
Lick-booting and *"ranka-de-de-izm"*
are pathways to the hearts of "great ones"
Secret-sucking of cancerous boobs
is money rain taking many to places
But they see and tell our world
upside-down

Eriata on Marble

Coming and going...
Running threads...
Crispy exchanges...

I love your loving hands...
Standing atop in all...

Simmers boil from pockets the world over
...smiles...faces...smiles...
fits and starts...

I love your loving hands...
Warm and caring...

Beat some sounds of love...
Sides to love will dance their sides
muddy grounds will stand as tests

I love your loving hands...
Assurance...awesome sweet...

Paved columns resonate with
charged moments of now
and tomorrow...to last and last?

I love your loving hands...
One to lean and lean...

Coming and going...
Boiling pockets...
Paved columns charged...

Love holds on?

Eriata Oribhabor

Power, Housing and Works will work as one.
In their separate ways,
they will go "*won-bai-won*"

Developed countries empty their energies
On Power, Works and Housing...
Petroleum Industry will drive the economy

The old will come as new
The new will in the newness of old
Run the race of old as new

When hands are fired to drive the state on
Template worn, lizards climb walls with
Ease of monkeys on trees

NEPA will rise again
National Shipping Line will rove our waters
Our airspace will house Nigeria Airways
From the sky, change will shower in changing ways

Today...

I will call my kit and kin to come and share my space for hope,
speak my heart and churn my bits in turns
and unbundle soothing peace in love pieces

Heavens will boom with sounds of happiness

Today...

Hands of hope will gather as one, walk the talk,
hound heads standing on truth for justice,
the Augean stable will stabilize and vestiges of pain will wash away

Convivial backslapping will change the color of our nagging aura

Today...

Remnants of darkness will crash like packs of cards,
uncommon brightness will grip lanes paved in scary emblems
and burdened hearts will flow with smiles reaching the skies

Heavens won't crash

Today...

Sorrow's ends will be pocketed in corners of confidence for better tomorrow,
rain of shame will cower at the audacity of rich crispy freedom
hearts will join for light

A world of peace will sit on palms

Today...

Eriata on Marble

Your appeal is a pillar of inspiration
Embedded in my every action

You come as hope
Shining in its boldness

Your lines are graded tonic wines
Not a day without a taste

On you, these lines run
On your tunes, they up

You hold spaces unknown
In you, I find a muse known

These lines running run for us
Blasting columns of hate

Touch my palm and feel my warmth
Commune large with boundless nature

Walk with me the hills of love
Dot our hearts with curvy kills

Read these lines and share as yours
Upon yours, they build and share

Roll back the pains you harbor
You are Creativity's Bus-stop

Eriata Oribhabor

The brightness of darkness has enveloped the hall
and the cry of state and nation is the lot of all

Light has traveled
No fuel in town

The ones running the show have gone for light,
women and men mope

How did we get here?

Darkness points a way,
light opens many ways
when a game starts without light,
brightness of darkness stands tall

This hall is full of life but the life of light is out.
We want to make success riding slap of darkness

There is no fuel in town
No crown to show in town

What path or pit are we headed
on crosses hoisted by hostage takers?

Eriata on Marble

I am coming to your city...
On reality table, shall we chew
on pockets of hidden talents,
In quarters close, shall we share
chat box tales,
At no cost, shall we un-box
reality waves

I am coming to your city...
On her love for poetry
and performances
shall we stroll,
On her audiences shall we
spell the name and color
of a people of cultural effrontery,
and wells of guarded history

I am coming from my city
with thousands to share
I am the taste of her rich
culinary mix making the round
in colors of national embrace,
I will pour on pounded yam;
a beautiful bride, soups fall over
for a stroll into bowels beyond...
Our knack for royal welcome
for visitors served natural drinks
in ringed calabashes, is given

I am coming to your city...

Eriata Oribhabor

The one running a birthday countdown
should wash the streets with waters of palm wine
and pound bowels with crafted goulashes

The one digging wells of gold
should plant silvers of golden colors in homes
and decorate jaded pavements with bronze railings
of hope

The one running errands for the gods
should pin kingly emblems on his forehead
showing retrogression
painted in light of progress
none will be fooled

The one who hounds the only palm tree in his
compound to death,
battles the affairs of life walking second fiddle
wherever palm wine kegs meet

The one parading spaces as a hawker of slippery
peels and killer stops,
plants mines of bombs of unwarranted holes for
generations

Eriata on Marble

Goal posts of success stand real
Sealed, awaiting feels

Life's taste comes sweet and sour
Thickets are never crickets of fried delicacies

The wind of poetry walks pass this way
A line train rails soothing images showing the way

The sound of poetic nomenclatures hoist colors of poetry
In its bowels, are hope, love and happiness

I commune with poetic spirits in their domains
And receive cups full of lines served in the best of poetic tradition

Yesterday, I drank from the well of peace
Uncommon music of inspiration reeled like of old

Old and new schools will cross their paths...
Holding a mix grill of yesterday and today

Not the speech rendered
Not the image laundered

All earned, wander not
All poached, not roaches

Eriata Oribhabor

Your cityscape is a given escape
Aura soothing for literary residences

Your people bask in a rich literary tradition
"Moni-mis-rod-dem" have no place in this station

My regrets are a legion run
The region of bad politics,

Your city's touch lies not in its spark of manicured lawns
But decency and fervency for a better tomorrow

Books speak crooks on streets naked
Building likes in place of tomorrow's pillars

Your sociocultural centre peaks high in all
Standing tall isn't a fall run on a broken glass

If the reign of awakening swallows the grass in us,
greenery would voice the us in us.

Let the weight of hope fire you up planes of
healthy endowments
Today, not tomorrow, will cherished paces run

Eriata on Marble

I found my rhythm tucked in my mother's garden
I pluck senses laden with motherly love

I found my poetic face painted cool
It draws from our village square embracing my inquisitive self without let

I found the waters of poetry in its rushing flow
A book of many colors, turns me an unceasing water-spitting pipe duck
dotting streets of cities as hope

I found a wand with a touch of class
A warm hug is a jug of tea gulped hot on beautiful corridors

I landed from the bottom of the bottom, to the top of the bottom holding through...
My first lines sealed, started blind as bottom lines for bottom lines

I found the key to freedom lines
Lined as pockets of great pages

I have found the page and the stage
I will run pages and build stages

They say spirits build mountains in the hills of our hearts
Mountains of moles stand as centurions on our ways

They say the one with peculiar knack for figure juggling
is a money safe in his own right destined to protect our leaking till
Figures climb on pages...tills boil over with fingerlings of corruption

The say the booth of life must be lined with hot cash to keep it warm at all times
Single Treasury Account will account the death of poor souls in the land

They say the best of weathers flows with bashfulness
A dash of wine they say, is good for hearts

The say the sign of the times is best read from thundering lines of the weather
Yesterday...it rained from the secrets of our backdoors

They say we run two seasons marked and none tempers the other's lane
I will tell you tales of weather diseases and weathering raves bursting lines and marked lanes of this world

Eriata on Marble

I build and run my lines on the streets of my head
headed for golden pages housed
Our paths watered with insightful linings

I hold my space and throw myself baby
Brackets of earned poetic pushes pour at hours odd

Your space runs in these lines...drink
The taste of pieces of broken glass will never take
its former self

I run with the contours of local spaces
In them I read the measure of our failures in great
measures

I play with the guitar of the flutist who taught me
the ways of pianos
in the home of a drummer singing in many tongues

I am coming with my band...
to rock the stages with uncommon sense of poetic
accoutrements

Let's meet at the town hall...
we shall rebuild its walls infested with cracks from
mis-governance
We shall sink new pillars for society

Where is REFINARY located on the oil map of this nation?
You will find it on a painted signboard touching the sky of oil and book capital

Where are the roads running on TV screens across our land?
Groundbreaking ceremonies made up for them

We are "blessed" with potholes and road "patchers"
A legion resides in the city of dirty beaches

Crossing the deepest dimensional lines of a Rubicon
isn't a spree of midnight drinking

The handwriting on the wall speaks large
Education runs reverse peaks of failure

Tell the Teacher to spell his name
He says; REFINARY and REFINERY are same

Eriata on Marble

Meeting points are crossroads
open for two and more;
making or marring...
Unique signage
hoisted

This meaning wasn't the reason
Not in the cards...not in their books
But the state of things simmered
In sweet burn fires of poetic
Cross-fires slowly drawing
From rich scented roots
Of budding acquaintance

The reason wasn't a selfish feeling
Of one out to run the other through
Not in the cards...not in their books
But when the run of things boomed
In witty exchanges, affection grew
In careful range of surprises
Only the matured, could
In sincerity handle

The reason wasn't a flash of affection
But the beginning of genuine bonding.
A private consummation wasn't in view
When showers of sweaty droplets
Turned a peaceful outcome,
A snuggle was in their cards

The reason was a meaning in a season

Eriata Oribhabor

Of bomb blasts and imploding rains,
Political mishaps, misfits and pain.
When the fear and noise of fixing
Common interests lost its hold,
Feelings of sincere affection
build for the bounties of
Genuine friendship

Eriata on Marble

Fifty is a magic number
I am at a crossroad of poetic musings

Bear my poetic hemorrhage...
It happens in a blue moon
Last seen in a cubicle
Across the oceans.
On that day,
I shed poetic tears
Of rainy lines

Fifty is a magic number
I am at a crossroad of poetic musings

Bear my poetic swings
They snap on me napping
In quiet naps.
In their last arrival,
I drank sweet confidence
In beaded lines

Fifty is a magic number
I am at a crossroad of poetic musings

Quest for glory is a run of steadfastness
Story to story comes story of stories
More than a coin in the pocket
All started from a coin

Every pillar is a coin
Every coin is a pillar

Eriata Oribhabor

If you spot my dance steps,
step to dance with me
If you hear my crying sounds,
come quick to stand for me
If you hold me dearly true,
watch with keen my back
If we hold through to these,
we will be on track

The mood of things will for us, shine
The us in us will blow and bloom
Doom of yesterday will drown in doom
The boom we yearn will shower as bliss for us

Climb the rope and take a mile
Wind your waist and beam in smiles
Not without your foes and friends
None comes to dine as fiend

Beat your chest and drum the story
Tell the ones your time would carry
Thorns and thickets will burn to ashes
Dance a dance to wrap the patches

All shall drink to embrace your past
In an envelope of the present,
Lend your present the teeth to bite
Stand and run on bright as light

Eriata on Marble

The Victory sign is up
Songs of yore and now are up
Stand with us to wine and dine
Just a way to say we are fine

The victory sign is up
Drums of war are drowned and down
Come with us to speak the way
Away from valleys of brimful worries

The victory sign is up
Up your game in all that's fair
Spare yourself the fate of pain
Away from the maddening sane

The victory sign is up
"kokoma" dance is all I know
Add the time and build a rhythm
Both will make a blend for all in time

The victory sign is up for good
The good of all and all for good
Pour some wine and wash your faces
These spaces are for you and me

The victory sign is up
Up-stand and join the top
Away from the bottom you left
For here we must stay and cleft

Eriata Oribhabor

Cock your mouth and run amok...spit on your people
Fart your way around your spaces...pour on them hot shit

Build an empire and walk on rivers...steal blind
And add pain to feverish homes...add some sugar

Stress the streets and rock your fortress
Raise domes of palatial feats and light your street...blank the rest

Build paradises, be busy...your spit will flow as rivers
Channeled on the paths of your opposition

Expand your empire...be deaf...mountains will in your name, rise
All will boast your ways with cultish pride...in your name, walk tall

Tell your people to "go to hell" - they made you not
Curse them...tell them power resides in your pockets

Get around and find your niche...you will reach heights towering large
Fund a band to dance on drums...novel stakes matter

You are the best thing "after the making of the

Eriata on Marble

king"
You hold the aces the king and all will turn.

You belong to the Centre
Your Corner will never be a Centre

These running lines will pass your door mouth
Bathe them colors fitting for the next stop

These promissory notes will stop at every stop lending voice to voices
Hewers of wood and drawers of water would find them handy

These leading lines run with running changes
Change agents have found a ground norm

Everything boils as politics
Poetry holds them all in poetic pieces

Who wants politics?
It maims and writes death sentences for many.

Whose politics do we stand to speak?
It is the farm yard of many families

When politics falls short of sweet for some, they wear it the toga of bitter
In all, we find it oozing from bedrooms across our land

I am not writing your poetry, not parodying your politics
I am moving across your fields speaking your filth in running lines for a better tomorrow

These lines will stand handy for all lands...

political gangs must retrace their dirty steps and
rewrite politics in fervency of societal uplifts

If politics isn't the good life,
The good life will wash away in tears

If poetry isn't the market of ideas
Ideas will die...never to wake up

Eriata Oribhabor

Have you seen my cover photo lately?
It tells the songs of victory and chords of success

Would you stay aloof or run with me?
Groan or pop Champaign with me?

Have you seen agents of your local authority clear your drains lately?
They speak coated-sugar tongues building shame

Would you stay aloof or run with me?
Bemoan your state or align with me?

Is today not the ruin wrought on us by them?
Is environmental sanitation not contracts gone bunkum?

Would you walk alone or join with me?
Stand debased by fiends that reign in lies?

Tomorrow is Sanitation day...sub-humans
will be hounded to sweep some sense
of humanity on their streets
Paid taxes cool off in foreign banks

Would you hang gagged or run with me?
Down and out or out to run with me?

Who wears the title of STUPIDITY?
Them and us faking in FERCUNDITY

Eriata on Marble

A great country bugged down by bed bugs
Count the blessings and see our pain

Did you see the moment in yesterday?
Did you chew from the kolanuts of true elders?

Would you join the line train at 57?
Mill-Runners come foisted by Godfathers

Would you be joining the run of the mill?
Or berth at the harbor of successful crafts?

The story will announce as one you knew
Remember, many are stewing in their broths

Where will you be when counted hands steer the ship of state?
Where will you be when razor sharped tongues lick their wounds?

Where will you be when change changes the changing faces of change?
Where will you be when the step and stops of life catch up with them?

Bed bugs…

Eriata Oribhabor

Festivals will populate our calendar like the popular use of "International" posted on signboards around our country but not all poetry events should international bear –
      not all events should festival wear

Roll out the events, roll out the moments, roll out the books for all to celebrate,
in them are pillars raised for today and tomorrow's good –
not all events should adorn the festival barge

Our state will bounce back in glories lost, our ways will draw not flacks but praise, our lack will wash, not grow; hearts will bubble in hues of positive memories running generations through

Bring back events, call them events, wear them names, shower them in poetic greases, give them teeth, crown them success gowns, let them stand tall in poetic imageries,
roll them local, blow them international,
let poetry be without local or international,
let poetry be, let festival be

Welcome to our world of local flavors matching international,
welcome to international pacing corners of our world, come savor our flavors; flavors standing spread in ways than one...
wine and shine abound in our land of bounties

Eriata on Marble

Where shall one walk the talk and fix lines of gaping ineptitude?

Where shall one stroll in open extol of tiny dots of positive forays?

When shall one's identity lay spread on the books of public opinion cracked?

When shall the sun's ray pour as waters of peace sweltering on our streets?

When shall the moon's calmness speak the aura we yearn?

What do we do from here? Who holds the stand we share to stand?

Can't you see my shyness?
I loathe to hug and kiss in secrets

Did you hear of my timidity of shame?
I dance in the open like them

I run from games that rub my hands in bribes
But laugh with bribes that come coded

Did you hear how many would make meaning on gifted lines?
All will run with running lines...rolled tight

Eriata Oribhabor

Someone said you were nominated for a literary
prize and your votes would count you carting home
a prize money worth two million Naira
    Your votes poured like the last rain raining
        "Mangoes and Oranges"
You coasted the victory shores with a huge scar
      still spinning in your memory

      Mum is the word
      All dead

Someone pleaded your brain to build words of
Foreword to steady a book for the international
audience. He direly needed to sound a good start to
        position his status
He needn't pay you a dime because it was an honor
to be recognized in a country of more than a 160m
    people. Foreword forwarded

      Mum is the word
      All dead

Someone came Liking and Tagging you beaming
    the newest support in town
He needed your time and energy to fashion way
forward for Forewords and Forwards unlocking the
key to Prize monies in conditions perfect and
      destinations real
    He read the lines and hid away

Eriata on Marble

Mum is the word
All dead

Someone recognizes your craft and painted the
skies bright on your innocent palms boasting
actions to ferry your people to the moon for the
gains of modernity kept away from your continent
of blind leaders
The content of his veins tastes like yours
Sun and moon is brighter here; you told him so

Mum is the word
All dead

At this season's peak, carpet of leafs will adorn our streets for free
All season foliage, shall host seasoned banters

Drums will roll for men of honor served cherished rum
Euphoria of yesterday shall serve our coast

On splendor streets of our minds, values lost shall be shared.
We shall bear witnesses for golden herbs cocooned by foreignness

Lost sheep will take agenda spaces
Panacea for helplessness will grip perspectives

Weathers come and go serving values they bear
So it was when communions shaded by foliage meant more

Eriata on Marble

Soon,
we shall be counting how we fared,
speak how we got imparted by activities around
lanes we ply extoling one holding the aces in all

Soon,
our domains will count in blessings swallowing odds
that never had their ways
when new lines like these run, many would willingly
launder how they got infected by the poetic bug, ever
contagious, ever inspiring

Soon,
the time we yearn would fall on our laps,
we shall clap the claps of joy over unhappiness,
sorrow and its painful associates; running tears would
never count with us

Soon,
eyes will speak and mouths would see the rhythm in
the drive for collective passions whisking us from
countryside to countryside,
city to city, stealing our comforts for perspective re-
engineering

Soon,
running efforts shall bring sweet gainful gains of
togetherness
and victory for stories perfect worth posting in fonts
of glorious bolds
These lines running are far reaching statements
stating all...

Eriata Oribhabor

I am sourcing the source of senses right making sense
In domains of sensibility found

The senselessness of senses on display is painted
in the color of senselessness
It lives with us

The pen in the centre of our political universe
is central in every sense
To be strongly held

Stuck between making a sensible statement,
I see modicum of senses built
Hearts of readers await

I have a message of senses burning in me
Find them pinned and locked.

Did I make any sense?
Where is my statement?

Today is Worship Day.
Make a statement of faith.
Make some sense and send a message.

Send a message of truthfulness
Make sense in every sense

Send messages of hope
Not bombs

Eriata on Marble

Where do you think this source is rooted?
I am experience sipped all over

Where did we last meet?
On a crossroad paved by potholes and patches of painful splashes;
"terrain of endless possibilities...

Where would we be tomorrow?
We shall meet where potholes and ruinous splashes open
in deepened shame
from "the field of our visions,
we shall watch visions realized"
in bright lights

Eyes shall awaken to negative deft pushed too far.
Where would we be?

When the fragrance of a coincidence tastes nice,
you want to drown and drown in it

When a road's aura serenades in openness,
you want to cling to it

When the coincidence of the call for poems on food
and photos of foods take the stage, you want to
jump at them

When a conference of photos on food and food
poetry holds,
a statement will paint our walls

When Men and Women of God address members
of their congregations in rhyming schemes, poetry
is given a boost

When the works of your hands click in fitting
finishing,
you bow your head in praise of Him that owns the
all in all

The weight of the gun is heavier than its languid carrier
banking on the day's tip to eke a squared living

Tips may trickle in from vexed faces...all waiting on leaders and government...government and leaders...no leaders, no government...
minimum wage needs a wedge

Community of street hawkers thrive...they know their ways with traffic wardens,
police, government approved touts (GAT)
hardened by the vagaries of the polity...
every government uses them to line their pockets with beautiful stones

Boxed faces are vexed; waiting for 18,000 Naira minimum wage

An umbrella seller huddles a car...
its occupant barely hears him...cats and dogs rain, "mangoes" and "oranges" pour...
no umbrella over the seller running around to square a living

Let's meet where the reign of value speaks...
where mountains stand as straight lines of meaning...
weaning credibility for sane paths

Eriata Oribhabor

Lamps are not forever shine
Faces fade, gloat and bloat

The King's son is a key pun
Not all engage in traditional runs

A waiting wait rests like a slate
A golden patience may open gates

The dog speaks in doggy ways
Clogs overtake our cranny ways

Not lines you pick on the streets
Hard times burn as beats birthing feats

A steak of fried "amala" will do
"Amala?" Where are you coming from?

Not shopping for whips of poetic lines
My running lines run ahead of wasted lines

I will whip you in line with today's lines
Are you one lost in foreign lines?

We shall meet on this at 69
69 isn't a perfect no

Eriata on Marble

He showed her his world on pages
written under a golden sun
bound on a land of green and white

Hers were printed letters flared
in fires lit by Spanish colonizers
landing across the West Atlantic side

Elegantly clothed in colors of old and rich
history...his stories rhymed in awe...
her's mostly versed free

She would listen to his accent
and get lost; while he wondered
around the gist of her mother tongue

Voices come from all directions
Poets and dreamers with fond intentions
Theirs were the words of recognition

The instant caught them looking yet
it missed the sound and the rest of the senses'
rumination on the newness of the other

Now, kept in lines and motioned witnesses
their poetry continue to become and behold
rounding it all, in timely interconnection.

Pilar R. Aranda

Eriata Oribhabor

Poet me,
poet you

Lost in lines of a poet loved,
grounds wet raise

Washed dry by deft and wit,
planted feats sow

Deep in lines of love found,
bonded ties settle

Sweet lines and wits sipped,
depth of fondness, is richness

A feel of feelings reel,
hearts of watering lines spill

These lines of you and me,
come from me and you

You, poet...me, poet
Poet, me...poet, you

pouring still on the 'rusty caps' of Ibadan
are poetic dusts from the Fist of Words
showered bold by gifted brains...
as lines of love and hope for all;
today's revolution -
better tomorrow

pouring still on the jaded streets of Ibadan
are lines of commitment and service
empowered to hold the aces
for fatherland...untie nutty reigns
of streets decorated by
wastes and shame

pouring still are the dusts of Fists of Words,
its rhymes and rhythms will haunt an ivory tower
finding feet to feed its lawns with free waters of love,
in search of formulas to fix her non-functional utilities...
if her booming stench from toilets don't stop,
where is decency we mouth?

pouring hard on hearts are worries
of reflating waning ways of a land
burnished on billboards as magical wands
of change and transformation...lacking freshness
promised on pages of newspapers and televisions -
pecks without specs

Eriata Oribhabor

if this revolution runs from the bottom of our hearts
and pumped on the streets, authorities will be ruffled
forgotten parts of pain and shame will join to build
a wining whole...collective tills will build again;
greenery of old will come in brightened forms
killing stenches of pain and shame...feeding souls

Eriata on Marble

If these words are deficient
of needed figures, let its rigors
form building blocks for the speech
building in your head on our first meet ,
when bread in warm conviviality
was shared over tea and coffee

If these words would smear
efforts shared on the square
of truth and equity,
way forward for words,
must climb the stairs
of confidence centers

If these words won't pay us
through labyrinths of wasted paths,
weave them stronger
as bridge-building perspectives
spiriting lack from plenty
fixing booms from lost booms

If these words didn't from a letter grow,
the sweat of dots, commas, colons
and their kit and kin would have
no place in the run of phrases
and sentences

If these words require an endorsement
from outer space, the moment's space

would be lacking in driving them
to needed spaces...
new line masons are crafting
tools for building millennial
reasoning...changing the game
in winning ways

If these words speak lies
of me and you in spiteful ways,
paint them aright in truth to stop
the norm of complacency,
and hands shall parade
the streets speaking
life to lines sitting
on pages large

Eriata on Marble

The game is out with a crown
familiar tones raft our town
ringing sounds of our forefathers
whose palms pounded drums
in calm clinical finishing

Women in bespoke apparels dance
their hearts, our souls and cadence
are memories of yore;
womanhood was Queen-hood
earned as bank of fidelity

The name is out in its finest test,
of earned heritage
consumed by the aura of cultural camaraderie,
the bar of humanity
raises in true meaning

Men roll in manly outpouring
drumming wars and victories won
adventures and success tales
upping society's oneness
eyeing the coming commingling

These lines ooze from mum's cooking pot made richer by handpicked contributions from our popular cow slaughter ground after hawking rounds

These lines build from drains and lawns of Warri from which my school fees was paid by an illiterate teacher whose hands dug deep building a town retracing her warm past lost to bungled values

These lines will flow in thousand depths of hard realities served hawking mum's "akara" and "agidi" before school time

These lines would spring momentary stops for a refresh of diverse pasts of rich reality lines...in collaboration, will capture today's yesterday across our spaces

Eriata on Marble

Eye brows raised
Dusts raised

Eye dusts?
Heard in a bus

Dust your eyes
Browse our slangs

Eye dusts?
Heard from a burst

sounds of poetry come
like a needle
in a haystack,
fathomed bright from cracks,
rounds of heart - pounds for joy
nothing to something
lack to plenty...

stories of poetry written come
as plenty from common lack
waters of plenteous gifts
and bounteous ways
commitment, courage
and molded drives,
sharpened aright

icing spread for caked souls
and wasted poles of hands
of complacency and revved
antidotes
for societal push
lifters of jaded spaces...

Eriata on Marble

I started out...many lines back
Been a long walk...looking back
Built bridges, crossing miles
My lot...

I started odd...thinking miles
Been crazy...reaching miles
Built champions, raising lines
My pluses...

I come as one on a horse back
Been rich...in awesome lack
Built lines...building packs
Running lines...

I started out...one word, one line
Been riding lines...great lines
Built columns...roof lines
My home...

I come as a wanderer...learning ropes
Been a wondrous journey...coping
Reaping nuts...writing hope
Lines of life...

Eriata Oribhabor

In humanity's home of scented greenery,
dotted palms of warm aromatic smiles
stand tall and run in bowels
of ordered colonnades

Sprinkles of harmless shower,
wash the feet of palms,
lawns of peace are breastfed
hope, poured on humanity's communion

Peace palpably drips from faces
Roots and colors hide in large cases
Multi-roots stand as tap roots
Breathing the streets as one big foot

Not the bemoaned of dirtied ways
Of disunity squeaking unity
Or, launderers of disunity lost
In costly flips of untamed blindness.

Eriata on Marble

www.ingramcontent.com/pod-product-compliance
Lightning Source LLC
Chambersburg PA
CBHW051348040426
42453CB00007B/471